PLANNING YOUR DREAM WEDDING

IN TUSCANY

BY: JENNIFER A. MARTIN

This book is dedicated to my family for their support throughout the years and allowing me to spread my wings and explore the world. Thank you to my husband for allowing me to fulfill my dreams and creating an indescribable wedding in amazing Tuscany. Appreciate the encouragement of Darby for the inspiration to write this book and Daniela for your insight to Tuscan wedding planning.

Table of Contents

Introduction to My Italian Heritage...1

Why Italy?...6

Getting Started to Plan Your Dream Wedding 9

Where in Tuscany to Get Married 12

Transportation...21

When to Get Married in Italy...24

Getting Married in Florence, Firenze 28

The Legalities 33

Types of Wedding Ceremonies 39

The Food of Tuscany..45

The Wines of Tuscany..50

Wedding Attire & Aethetics...54

Musical Offerings 59

Selecting a Photographer 62

Choosing a Florist 65

Introduction to My Italian Heritage

Little did I know growing up in an Italian family where it would have led me to today. Both my mother and father are of Italian descent. My great grandparents came over from Italy in the early 1900's so my grandparents grew up learning Italian, but my parents never learned it to transfer their knowledge to me. Italian was the language spoken in the household only when they didn't want my parents, whom were young at the time, to exactly know what they were saying. I can do that now in my own house, but being the only person that knows how to speak Italian I don't know how exciting that would be to talk to myself.

Growing up I came from a good sized family and felt that we were always together celebrating holidays, birthdays or just because. One thing that there was never a shortage of in our family was food. Who would've figured that Italians love to eat? My mother is an amazing cook and had learned from her Italian grandmother. I love to cook myself, but in this day in age finding the time to put aside to make the sort of meals that I want to make is difficult every day.

I didn't fully appreciate my culture until the year I studied abroad in college in the fall of 2001. I actually left the week before the tragic 9/11 took place. Talk about being in a foreign place and not knowing what to do. I had studied abroad for about four months in Florence, also known as Firenze, at the school of Lorenzo de Medici. To this day, signing up for that program was the best thing that I could've chosen to do in my life. Not only did it allow me to deepen my appreciation for my Italian roots, but I explored the rest of Europe and experienced a variety of other cultures including the food, traditions and landscapes of beautiful countries. Everything is a hop, skip and a jump when living in Europe by plane or even the train system. An overnight train is a good option as well.

I was now living in a foreign country with this being my first time overseas. I didn't know anyone, didn't speak the language, and was starting to wonder what I got myself into. I wasn't the only one in this boat as other students arrived and as we all got to know one another, we started exploring and traveling. With cramming all my school classes into 3 days, it gave me the rest of the week to explore Italy and other countries. I was amazed at the end of our stay how many people didn't take advantage of the time and didn't even experience what not only Italy, but Florence had to offer. I never took a minute for granted and when I wasn't in classes, I was roaming the city exploring all the small streets, shops and admiring the eye-opening architecture. There were days I even jumped on a Sita, intercity bus, and went to a random Tuscan town and walked around watching the locals interact or admired the local craftsmanship of the products sold.

Those four months flew by and I wanted to stay another semester, but I didn't have enough electives to take additional classes there and I wouldn't have graduated on time. I wanted to work over there after graduation, but couldn't find a job or a company in the US with Italian offices. I found myself in a situation where I had a desire to be there, but couldn't leave my family. I felt that I left a part of me in Florence. Upon my return I felt even more family oriented and wanted to get my family together more often since life is s short. I brought back no only memories, but lessons in the true Italian way of life.

To keep myself involved with what I had experienced, I started taking classes with a fantastic Italian teacher, who runs the Italian Program in the heart of Boston's "Little Italy". Through the program, I met other like-minded folks that had been to Italy, had a love for it and wanted to learn the language or were of Italian heritage and wanted to brush up on what they learned growing up.

One of the things that I came to appreciate while living in Italy was wine. Quite a change from only liking Carlo Rossi and Arbor Mist while in college. Living in Tuscany I, of course, got forced into jumping right into reds, since this is the majority of wine in this region. Every region I visited, while traveling throughout Italy, had such fantastic food and wine that paired so well together. I loved that every region had their own culinary specialties and traditions. It was always exciting going to visit to a new region and to have all this world famous wine at your finger tips or even within a drive just to visit the winery yourself was a dream.

I came to appreciate wine more as the years went on by visiting the Finger Lakes wine region in upstate New York and attending numerous tastings and events throughout the Boston area. I had a feeling that one day I would want to be involved in the business so I started working part time for one of Massachusetts biggest wine importers at their retail wine shop in the Italian section of Boston, the North End, and later another local wine shop as a sales consultant for a small Italian wine importer. That all came to an end when I bought a home and moved further away from Boston.

Still to this day, fourteen years later, I remain involved every day with the Italian world. Almost two years ago, after putting all my energy into studying the Italian language for five years, I had lost focus on the wine world, which led me to begin writing an Italian wine blog called <u>Vino Travels</u>. I started Vino Travels to promote mostly the small and medium sized producers throughout all twenty wine regions of Italy that are producing great wines from many of the native grapes throughout Italy that folks may not be aware of. Since the producers all had such great wine and history behind them, I felt I should share this with the world. I also wanted to educate folks on the variety of grapes to make them less intimidating while searching for wines. In the end, it's all about drinking. Do I need to twist your arm?

On my site, I like to incorporate my travel in Italy throughout my stories when I can and sometimes provide food suggestions depending on what is typical of the region I'm discussing. My blog allows me to communicate with folks throughout Italy and the world discussing food and wine of the twenty regions. From the years of traveling throughout Italy and meeting some top Italian food, wine and travel bloggers, I ended up getting involved in marketing all-inclusive guided tours to Italy to a number of regions including Tuscany, Puglia, Piedmont, etc.

My journey started from living abroad to where I am today. Nothing takes the cake to fulfilling a dream until my wedding in Italy. Thinking back, it all started with a study abroad program in college. I wrote this book because I really enjoyed planning our wedding in Italy and wanted to encourage folks abroad that it's possible to do it yourself without a wedding planner and to take pride in planning your wedding from start to finish. In addition, the cost savings is a definite plus. I hope you find this book to be your comprehensive guide to get your wedding plans kicked off and achieved from the comfort of your own home. I'm always happy to offer additional advice and questions once you're done reading this book, so feel free to shoot me an email at vinotravels@hotmail.com. Enjoy and good luck on your wedding adventure!

Why Italy?

You're probably reading this book because you have your own personal attachment to Italy and have chosen Italy for your wedding day. Maybe you haven't figured it out yet and are trying to narrow down a selection to a particular country as to where you want to celebrate a destination wedding. I have traveled to many countries in Europe and the world and there is a reason why Italy is one of the top destinations for folks in terms of vacationing and those that choose to uproot and live there permanently. The people, the food, the wine, the history, the architecture, the beauty of its varied topography and the overall lifestyle. The list goes on my friends.

You may ask where the idea of getting married in Italy come from for me. Yes, I lived there for a short period, but did I meet an Italian man that swept me off my feet? No, but I tried when I studied there years and years ago. In just four months of living there, I knew that I wanted to return to Italy one day when I did meet "the one" and get married there? I absolutely knew! Those four short months of living there and experiencing what an amazing country it is and how much the Italians appreciate life and family was all it took. The way food and wine unite people in that country is harmonious. What was intriguing to me was how each region was so different and had so much to offer for a variety of tastes. After all my experiences throughout Italy, I was even more proud to have ancestors that originated from such an amazing place.

So yes, after living in Florence and falling in love with that city and the whole country, I knew that I wanted to go back and get married there one day. If you have experienced it yourself, you already understand and if you haven't yet you are in for such a treat. For myself it wasn't just a feeling of traveling and saying to yourself what a beautiful place this is. When I left Florence I had this feeling I left a part of me behind and whenever I went back I always felt like I was home. It was an indescribable feeling, but just like when you meet the right person you just know, well I just knew!

If you have had friends that have already gotten married, you may have experienced what I had from watching them go through the wedding process. It was always shocking to me how my friends couldn't wait for their wedding day to be over. Who wants to plan something from 6 months to 2 years, depending on how long your engagement is, which is supposed to be the happiest day of your life, but you can't wait for it to be over? Not me! I wanted to get away from that madness and get back to the reason why folks actually get married. Did we forget what weddings are all about? It's the love and marriage of one couple who want to spend the rest of their lives together and celebrate it with their loved ones. It's not who has the best wedding, who can show off the most, spend the most money, etc.. At least it wasn't for me.

Once you have discovered that Italy is the place that you want to get married there is so much to consider. All your options and choices depend on many factors. Your first question should be whether you want to do it yourself as I did with a little assistance or do you want to get a wedding planner for the whole thing? We are going to cover this and many of these topics throughout this book to help you along your way and save money in the process of doing it yourself. If I can figure it out and plan it myself, you can too! Hang on for the ride. I'll be your personal wedding guide through the process. I'm also willing to help and offer assistance once you've read through the book at my email vinotravels@hotmail.com. It was my dream and I enjoy offering tips to make your dream a reality too.

Getting Started to Plan Your Dream Wedding

You have two options in incorporating Italy into your wedding plans. Option one is to take the tasks of legalities out of the way by legally getting married in your home country and following it up with the ceremony and celebrations in Italy. Otherwise, option two is to go all in and complete the full legal services and ceremony in Italy as I did. Hopefully this book will give you enough guidance and instill some confidence so that you can carry out option two on your own or with a little assistance.

The extent of your wedding planning depends on the expectations you have set for yourself and what you value. Do you want it formal or informal? Is it going to be a large wedding with folks flying in from all over the world or small and intimate? Obviously, the more detail you want the more planning and research it will take, but everything is possible.

First things first, how do you even begin to plan a wedding in Italy? Where do you start? Can it be done on your own without a wedding planner? Of course it can! Technology is so sophisticated today that everything is possible to do from your home including planning your own wedding in a foreign country. The resources that we have access to now-a-days is insurmountable. We have online translators for documents, skype to virtually meet folks over the internet for free and search engines to answer any and every question you can possibly imagine as well as search for your vendors. Don't forget companies like Paypal that help protect both parties when it comes to payments.

Do I hire a wedding planner?
You may get to a point in the process where you feel comfortable planning most aspects, but maybe not others. You still have the option to hire and engage a wedding planner for a part or two depending on how much trust you have in yourself and your selections. Granted, this book is about planning your own wedding, but if you plan half or the majority of your own

wedding, then you have already drastically reduced the total cost.

At any point you feel you'd like the assistance of a wedding planner, I strongly recommend <u>The Tuscan Wedding</u> owned and operated by Daniela Tripodi. Daniela is a reputable wedding planner and her passion for wedding planning is evident in the customer service she provides to her brides. At the very end of planning I added an element to our wedding that I hadn't even thought about, transportation. I researched some vendors directly and the overall price Daniela provided was the best. It wasn't just the price as it was Daniela's quick responses and her demonstrated ability to be over the top with communication. You can't ever communicate enough going through this process. She even followed up with our accommodations to make sure everything was all taken care of with our shuttle. She even got an additional discount refunded to us from the company for a small hiccup that day. If you use Daniela please let her know I sent you. We've even kept in contact and have become friendly. You too will probably if you get to know her and use her services.

Resources

Fortunately, I have traveled to many countries so far in my life and have planned everything myself. A couple of resources that have always proved to be invaluable for me are Trip Advisor and your favorite travel guide, mine is Frommers. These resources are jam packed with information with overviews of regions, places to visit, accommodations, attractions and restaurants.

Trip Advisor is very user friendly and easy to navigate. The best feature of Trip Advisor are the reviews as this will speak volumes about locations, attractions, restaurants and vendors. Typically I recommend searching from the top rated establishments in the cities or villages that you are looking for information from and search down from there, but make sure that they are rated highly on a large number of reviews rather than one or two. Sometimes places might have a high ranking, but have a limited amount of reviews. Other vendors may be placed a couple rankings below, but may have a larger amount of reviews that are obviously much more valuable.

Now is the time to get into the nitty gritty and determine the where, when, how and all the extras in between.

Where in Tuscany to Get Married

Located in the central heart of Italy, the region of Tuscany is best known for the birthplace of Italian renaissance. It's a region with a hilly terrain, medieval Tuscan towns rich in history with stunning architecture. It offers delicious Tuscan cuisine and some of Italy's highest rated wines. Its capital Florence, also known as Firenze, is rich with artistic and medieval history, while its borders extend west to the coast of the Tyrrhenian Sea with towns including Pisa, Carrara and Lucca to the northwest down to the marshlands of the Maremma and Grosseto to the south. Italy has something for everyone whether you love the sea, mountains, beaches, hills, cities or the countryside. It's all there. All this combined with its rather mild, continental weather makes Tuscany as one of the perfect places for your dream Italian wedding.

What drove you to pick Italy? Was it somewhere you also had lived or was it an area that you vacationed in and fell in love with? Maybe you have never been to Italy and have always wanted to go. If you have never gone, I definitely recommend a trip prior to the wedding to give you a sense of place, but it's not required. My choice in selecting a location was rather easy. I tossed with the idea of getting married in Florence, since I always pictured myself getting married there from my days of living there, but I wasn't sure I wanted to be surrounded by a bunch of tourists and chaos. Instead, I searched for somewhere in the countryside and ended up in the small town of Bucine where all my wedding guests could reside at for the week and base ourselves out of. I had a good friend that I had met when I lived in Florence and have remained friends throughout the years. I asked for his advice if he knew of any beautiful places to relax at for the week. After reviewing a few of the choices online and researching reviews, I knew it when I saw it. I chose to stay at the lovely Borgo Iesolana in Bucine (pictures included) and therefore, we decided to get married in the very small town of Bucine in Tuscany within the province of Arezzo.

If you have no recommendations and are starting from scratch, first think about the type of setting you want for your wedding. Do you want to be based in vineyards, coastal beaches, mountains, lakes, the ocean or sea, big city or a small town? The possibilities are endless! Italy has everything to offer for every wish and desire. Maybe you choose to get married in one of the hundreds of vineyards within Tuscany. If you love the ocean, there is the Cinque Terre that I'll discuss along with some of the Tuscan islands, including Elba.

Tuscany is dominated mostly by hills and coastal towns than mountains. If mountains are truly what you seek, you may want to take a look outside of Tuscany to northern Italy in the Italian Alps either around the Dolomites or up around the region of the Valle d'Aosta or even Trentino-Alto Adige. I've stayed in the Valle d'Aosta and as you enter the valley, the steep mountainous slopes surround you with views of the Italian Alps and the tallest mountain in western Europe, Monte Bianco, in the distance. It will take your breath away. As you get closer to the Italian Alps it feels as though they are literally hanging over you. This is a very picturesque area and one of the most stunning places I have personally been to in Italy.

Personal favorite Tuscan towns
Everyone has their favorite Tuscan town they have visited, want to visit or you've dreamed about getting married in so it's hard to really say which one would be best as it's all a matter of personal choice. The capital of Tuscany, Florence, is an obvious choice for many brides and I will solely focus on that in its own chapter, but if you choose to have something different, more intimate and away from the crowds, I'm going to highlight my personal favorite Tuscan towns that you should consider.

Fiesole – A small town a few miles outside of Florence perched up on the hill overlooking the Florence skyline. A pleasant, small town that allows you to take a step back in time to the Etruscans through its evidence of ancient ruins.

Montalcino & Montepulciano – Located in the Val d'Orcia the towns of Montalcino and Montepulciano offer some of Italy's finest wines in this south-western part of Tuscany. There are plenty of vineyards in this area and my choice of the two towns to consider would be Montepulcianano. Be ready to hike up hill as this town is set about 2,000 feet altitude, but the picturesque small alleys and Piazza Grande, once you've reached the top of the town, are all worth it.

Elba – One of the larger islands off the coast of Tuscany in the Tuscan archipelago reachable by ferry.

Cortona – One of my favorites! Live your own dream of "Under the Tuscan Sun" in this steep, perched town with sweeping panoramic views over the valley. Wander off the main street of Via Nazionale to be rewarded with what makes this town special and sit along the wall and catch a sunset or two.

Pienza – A compact town with a Renaissance flair and a great place for something more intimate.

San Gimignano – Known for its number of 13th and 14th century towers that surround the town once created by noble families.

Siena – One of the most popular of Tuscany's medieval towns with narrow streets and alleys. Plenty of attractions here from Siena's gothic Duomo to Piazza del Campo, which is Siena's main fan shaped charismatic piazza (square).

Volterra – Known for its alabaster, Volterra is a smaller sized town with plenty of rustic charm and character.

Pisa – Its main attraction is the Campo dei Miracoli, Field of Miracles, situated on the Piazza del Duomo, where the Leaning Tower of Pisa is located along with some other main attractions.

Lucca – A fortressed town, known for its wall that surrounds the historic center, where you can walk up above and admire the city below. Folks enjoy riding on bikes and strolling along the promenade.

Cinque Terre – Although not officially part of Tuscany, it's actually part of the region, Liguria, that borders Tuscany. For those of you that are looking to get married along the sea, this is a great destination. The Cinque Terre, meaning "five lands", consists of 5 delightful villages that stretch along cliffs on the Ligurian Sea. They're all connected by quick train rides or are most famous for their walking trails from one town to the next from easy to more advanced trails. For a picturesque backdrop of the blue seas and beaches and towns clustered along the sides of the mountains, this is your spot in Tuscany. Maybe your choice would be to get married on one of the beaches.

Hopefully, one or more of the towns that I've suggested have appealed to you since they are all my favorites for one reason or another from large to small. Once you've selected the town where you'd like to have your wedding, your next selection would be where within the town you would like to have your wedding. Depending upon which one of the three ceremonies you choose may dictate, to a certain degree, where you get married. For example, if you choose a religious ceremony this may be restricted to which churches will marry you in that town. If you choose a civil ceremony, you may choose to get married at the town hall. Otherwise, you can get married at a specific venue or villa for a civil ceremony or religious ceremony. I discuss all this in another chapter.

Types of Accomodations to consider

Where will you also be basing yourself and your guests throughout your stay? If you are staying in larger towns or cities, there are always the options of hotels. If you are out in the countryside, you can choose from private villas where the entire wedding party can stay together in one place. There are also other places to get accommodations at such as a tenuta, which is a family estate near a small village, or also an agriturismo, which are working farmhouses. In both of these options, guests can each have their own private apartments or rooms, but it still keeps the wedding party and guests all in one location depending on the size.

I truly enjoyed staying in an agriturismo and felt that you get a much more personal experience as usually the family themselves live onsite. Typically they use a lot of their own farm products for breakfasts or dinners as well. It can be quite the enjoyable experience and very affordable. I have used www.agriturismo.net and www.agriturismo.it in seeking out options within Tuscany as it is easy to navigate and provides reviews also. I also reference the name of the place with Tripadvisor as well as there are many more reviews there to refer to.

Transportation

Arriving from the airport

You may want to consider your location in proximity to ease of transportation to a major airport for yourself and your guests. The closer you are to a major airport or major city, the easier it will be for your guests to travel to and from the wedding. The two major airports in Tuscany are Florence 's Aeroporto A. Vespucci known as Peretola (FLR) and Pisa's Aeroporto Galileo Galilei (PSA). There are other airports that you could consider based on your travel plans before or after your wedding and whether your guests will want to travel before or after themselves that you could offer as suggestions. Rome largest airport, Leonardo da Vinci (FCO), also known as Fiumicino, is about two and a half hours from Florence. Be careful when suggesting Rome as there is more than one airport to consider. You can also consider the airports in the region of Emilia-Romagna to the north. In the town of Bologna there is Bologna Guglielmo Marconi Airport (BLQ) less than 2 hours from Florence. There is also in the region of Umbria to the east, the town of Perugia, with the San Francesco d'Assisi International Airport (PEG) also around a 2 hour drive away. Maybe you even start or end in Venice and Milan's airports that are more like 3+ hours train rides away from Florence.

Your final location will determine how folks want to arrive at their destination for the wedding after whether it's via a car, bus or Italy's fantastic train system. If you're choosing a major city or town you most likely can use the train system or public transportation to get there. If you choose a smaller town it will be more difficult to arrange public transportation for your guests without switching trains or buses, therefore, a car service or shuttle may be easier unless your guests want the ability to rent a car for their convenience.

Italy's train system is easy to figure out and you can look up train tickets in advance for the time schedule as well as purchase them online so you don't have to deal with the train stations and purchasing tickets there. Go to Tren Italia's website to purchase your tickets and view time tables. At the major airports and even the smaller ones you'll find some of your top car rental services including Avis, Hertz, Auto Europe and National. Look at the airport's website prior to know which rental agency you should make a reservation for.

The Day of your wedding

The level of detail in planning transportation for yourself and your guests is determined by your selected location. For example, you may be staying in the center of town and getting married there as well requiring the least amount of planning when it comes to transportation. For my wedding, I had to arrange transportation as we were on the outskirts of the center of a small town. One of the important aspects of our wedding for me was making sure I had a shuttle to take us through the Chianti Classico region for pictures ending up in Florence for sunset. Originally, I considered having folks use their car rentals, but I wouldn't turn back to that idea now knowing how wonderful it was for everyone to jump in the shuttle and be taken on a tour of Tuscany for the day enjoying the day without worries. If you have a large wedding with many guests, depending on your budget, one shuttle won't be enough so you may want to consider folks carpooling to the ceremony if there are enough car rentals to be utilized.

There are many options to consider whether you choose a limo, antique cars, a shuttle van, horse drawn carriages, a bicycle for two or maybe even a Vespa depending on how adventurous you are in your wedding dress. I don't personally recommend the company we used because the shuttle broke down at one point and they got a backup to replace it. A little hiccup for the day, but you want to try and avoid all worries as much as possible. Daniela Tripodi of Tuscan Weddings recommends Giotto Bus. Whichever company you select make sure to ask if there are any extras like gas, tolls or the fees that they must pay to enter certain cities. For example, Siena costs about 110 euro for the shuttle to enter for the day and San Gimignano was about 70 euro. You don't want any surprises so make sure to get an all-inclusive cost.

When to Get Married in Italy

How much time are you giving yourself to plan this wedding? I got engaged on 12/12/12 and we got married on 10/10/13 so I had 10 months to plan our Italian wedding. I also planned a reception for when we got back to celebrate with friends and other family members. It's very doable even if you only have 6 months or less, but every step is very important and you must not miss one, especially when it comes to the legalities and paperwork, which we will cover.

Weather

Weather is obviously a big factor to consider, especially for a wedding. We don't love the heat so the summer was automatically out for us. To catch the best weather conditions in Tuscany, the spring or summer will be your nicest weather, but autumn can be very nice as well with warm days and cool nights. Typically the spring and fall are less busy than the summer meaning less tourists and lower rates. Here is an overview of the seasons in Italy, but it's hard to generalize them as the south and north have very different temperatures as you can imagine.

- The summers in Tuscany are usually dry, very sunny and very hot. The summer months of July and August are also the busiest, meaning prices are at their highest. Keep in mind too that not all of Italy has air conditioning. Make sure if you choose the summer months for your wedding that you ask your venue and accommodations if they have air conditioning.
- Much of the inland and hilly areas have a more continental climate where rain is more likely as opposed to the coastal areas that are typically more Mediterranean.
- The fall months of October and November may have more rain, but still you'll have many dry days and they are typically less busy and warm, not hot. The Tuscan landscape is also extremely colorful during this time. October is one of my favorite times to travel to Italy.
- Winter in Tuscany can have sunny and mild days, but the

nights and days can sometimes get very cold. Be careful, depending on your location, if you aren't in some of the larger cities since some businesses may close for the winter, especially seaside towns. If you're in northern Italy in the Alpine regions at this time it can be high season with all the winter sports including skiing.

Holidays

As with all traveling, Holidays, celebrations and major events in Italy should definitely be on your radar when planning in order to avoid offices being closed or busy times for trying to make reservations throughout your stay. My suggestion is to first pick the time of year that you'd like to get married and with that information select your venue. Before committing to your venue, ask them if there are any particular holidays celebrated around the time of your wedding that would affect any travel plans or the day of your wedding just to be on the safe side.

August is prime time for the Italians themselves to vacation, known as *Ferragosta,* and it's amazing how much of the country closes down so keep this in mind. Responses will be slower during this time so do your best to get answers before and after. Throughout all of Italy, you may want to avoid Holy week in March and Easter as many places are closed and celebrations take place everywhere. For example, in Florence on Easter Sunday they have the "Scioppo del Carro", known as the Explosion of the Cart, where during mass at the Duomo doves are released and there are explosions outside in the piazza. The town of Siena, for another example, hosts the Palio in the months of July and August, which is a horse race where the local *contrada*, wards of the city, compete. Individual towns and cities will also host celebrations to honor their patron saint. For example, in Florence, June 24th is a big celebration for St. John the Baptist, the patron saint of Florence. It's all whatever you fancy and maybe you enjoy this excitement, but if you are not one for crowds these holidays and events should be considered because they may present some challenges.

Details for your guests

Once you have shaken out some of the details as to where and the timeframe of when you're getting married in Italy, you'll want to make sure to give your guests plenty of notice about when your wedding will be taking place. This is particularly important for weddings abroad, as it is likely that your guests will have to book some time off work as well to make necessary travel arrangements. Plus, with the cost of flights consistently on the rise, some folks may need to budget so that they can share your special day with you. Who wouldn't want an excuse to go to Italy, nevermind to attend a wedding of those they love?

Once you have the date and location locked down, send out your save the date cards as soon as possible. Even informally, until you get the save the dates, you may want to consider making it known with some calls or send out some emails to make sure everyone can get that timeframe in their calendar, as soon as possible. There will be a lot of information that folks will begin to request of you, but at least solidifying the date with them while letting them know that details are to follow will help. Now-a-days, wedding websites are very popular and very easy to create online. I used The Knot for creating a wedding website and it was very easy to navigate and setup and you don't have to be a technie to do so. This will give your guests a source of reference with live updates at all times and make your life easier. Make sure to mention the site in your invitations and save-the-dates.

This is the biggest item for your guests to pay attention to. I strongly recommend they check their passports for what their expiration dates are. Even though they may think that their passport will be valid for the time they'll be in Italy for the wedding, Italy requires a certain amount of time still valid on one's passport to enter into the country. For United States passport holders, it is required to have at least 3 months left on your passport, but the conservative side of me would go with 6 months to be on the safe side. Always verify this information with your country's embassy, as information can always change.

Getting Married in Florence, Firenze

The capital of Tuscany, Florence is one of the top most visited cities within Italy and has captured the hearts of many of those that have traveled to it. I personally love this city not only because of my bias for living there, but many other travelers around the world list Florence as one of their top favorite places in Italy. It's a perfect place for weddings with its monumental sites and buildings, intricate architecture and its historic city center, *centro storico,* is rather compact and easily walkable (although it's a little tricky in heels on the cobblestones as in many of the towns and cities throughout Italy).

Florence is a city rich in art and architecture including my ultimate highlight of the city, the Duomo. The Duomo's enormity and dimensions of architecture are breathtaking.

Duomo

There are plenty of other churches as well, including Santa Croce and Santa Maria Novella if they strike your fancy. Piazza Signoria hosts the Palazzo Vecchio with the replica of Michelangelo's David and a number of statues in the Loggia dei Lanzi. A popular wedding site within the city, where civil ceremonies take place, is at the Sala Rossa, or Red Hall, room within the Palazzo Vecchio. Once housing the governor of Florence, Baron Riccasoli Bettino, over 150 years ago, it's richly embellished and lavish décor provide an elegant setting for your ceremony.

Palazzo Vecchio

The oldest and historical bridge along the Arno River is the Ponte Vecchio that provides a riverside colorful backdrop. The Ponte Vecchio separates the historic center from the other side of the Arno River known as the Oltarno. This is where you will find the Boboli Gardens, at the Pitti Palace, if you are looking for something with more greenery and gardens in your pictures.

Ponte Vecchio

One of the top photographic attractions for brides and for all good reason is the panoramic shot of the Florence skyline that is highly recommended from Piazzale Michelangelo. It provides the best view over all of Florence. All the major historical monuments and structures stick out of the backdrop like a sore thumb. San Miniato, a nearby church to Piazzale Michelangelo, also overlooks the city and is another option that will probably be less crowded for pictures.

Piazzale Michelangelo

Besides the main attractions of the city, just the medieval streets alone provide an opportunity for the charm and character of the city itself. Your photographer that you end up selecting, has more often than not done photo shoots in Florence and may even have some hidden gems or nooks, as mine did for unique picture opportunities.

The only downfall about Florence, in comparison to some other smaller scaled Tuscan towns, are the crowds. We personally finished our day with our photographer for sunset at Piazzale Michelangelo with a last stroll through the streets of Florence. There were people everywhere, but they do clear the way for you and it even gives you an opportunity to live the life of the famous as I've never heard congratulations in so many languages and have never had so many pictures taken at one time. It's like the paparazzi were following us. If this is something you are comfortable with, you can have a lot of fun with it.

Piazza della Repubblica

The Legalities

The actual legalities of getting married in Italy is so important, but is the most daunting and nerve racking part. The last thing you want are for you and all your guests to be in Italy for the wedding, but due to missing a document or skipping an important step in the process, it will make it difficult or even impossible to fulfill the needs for that special day. Organization and attention to detail is key in this aspect of the wedding planning process. I'll share with you the steps as an American getting married in Italy, but always, ALWAYS, reference the Italian Consulate in your home country and their rules, since rules and laws can change at any time.

The timing of when all these documents are filed, processed and received are crucial to pay attention to, as some documents are only valid for certain periods of time. If you're like me and like to try and get things achieved in advance, this will not pay off. Patience is key throughout this part of the process.

The best way to tackle the legality process is to create a checklist. Make sure all documents are stored and kept in a safe place. It doesn't hurt to have copies of the documents as well. The information I'm providing to you was taken off of the USA Embassy's site and is the information for US Citizens to get married in Italy. Information changes and town halls have different rules depending on where you live so please make sure to use this only as a guide. Verify with both the town in Italy in which you plan to get married as to what their requirements are as well as your own town hall in your home country. They will be the ones to verify the documents and assert that you are legally married within your home country upon your return.

Here are guidelines for the paperwork requirements to get married in Italy. For full guidelines you should always contact an Italian Consular Officer in your country and/or the City Registrar (Ufficiale di Stato Civile) of the city where the marriage will occur in Italy.

Any foreigner that wishes to get married in Italy will need the following documents:

- A valid **U.S. passport** (always check how long beyond your length of stay your passport needs to be valid for , e.g. 6 months) or if you are a member of the U.S. Armed forces, a **military ID** is also acceptable
- **Original birth certificate** and long form is typically preferred. This must be translated by an official interpreter where you live and officialized with an apostille, which I will discuss in a bit.
- If you were married previously, you will need documentation of the termination of previous marriage(s). A female with a marriage terminated in the last 300 days must obtain a waiver from the Italian District Attorney's Office at the court of the city in Italy where the new marriage is performed. You also must prove that you aren't pregnant at the time in order to have a waiver released.
- Obtain the *Atto Notorio*. This document states that there are no obstacles for your marriage in the United States. This document is only valid for 90 days so be careful when you do obtain it. To obtain this document at your local embassy you must have two witnesses, non-related, go with you with their ID and sign the document in front of the consulate. If you are to receive it in the US or your home country, this will also need to be translated by an official interpreter. Personally I feel the more you can handle in your country prior to leaving for Italy the better. If you do choose to do it in Tuscany, you can obtain it at:
  - <u>**Florence Court House (Tribunale Ordinario)**</u>
    Viale Giudoni, 61
    Entrance B Floor 3 Room 102
    Phone:(+39)055-799-6880; 055-799-6451
    Hours: Monday-Friday 9:00am-12:45pm; Tuesday 3:00-5:00pm by appointment only. Inquires can be made Monday-Friday 12:00pm to 2:00pm.
    Email:volontariagiurisdizione.tribunale.firenze@giu

stizia.it
Site: http://tribunale.firenze.fsegiustizia.it/?i=230-1

- Obtain an affidavit sworn statement, known as **"dichiarazione giurata**" and ***Nulla Osta.*** This is presented to an American consular officer commissioned in Italy that states that there aren't any impediments to the marriage according to the laws within the United States or wherever you may be a resident. It basically grants you permission to get married in Italy. It should be obtained at least 3 days prior to the wedding. This is valid for 6 months only so preparing well in advance with this particular document will do you no good as it may not be valid by the time you get there. There is a $50 fee associated with this to be paid in cash. You both will need to go through security upon arrival. You can book your appointment online at https://evisaforms.state.gov/acs/default.asp?postcode=FLR&appcode=1.

  For Tuscany, the dichiarazione giurata/Nulla Osta form that you must print out and complete can be found at the following link: http://photos.state.gov/libraries/italy/217417/pdf/Marriage NullaOstaFlorence.pdf.

  Be aware to not sign the form until you are actually in front of the Consulate. They should have extras as well when you get there, but it's always better to have everything prepared in advance for these appointments. You will bring this form to the US General Consulate in Tuscany, which is located in Florence along the Arno River at:
  - **US General Consulate in Florence**
    Lungarno Vespucci, 38 – 50123 Florence
    Telephone (+39) 055-266-951
    Fax: (+39) 055-215-550
    Site: www.florence.usconsulate.gov

If you are marrying an Italian native, have them contact the Italian Embassy for what is needed.

- Once the affidavit or dichiarazione giurata has been received, you must proceed to the legalization office, ufficio legalizzione, at the **local prefettura** (Italian government office) in Italy. Prior to attending the prefettura, you must receive a stamp (**marca da bollo**) for 16 euro that can be purchased at any local tobacco shop, *tabacchi,* which are located in many places throughout every town and city in Italy. You can locate it by its sign that shows a blue letter T. Bringing that stamp with your other documents to the prefettura will authenticate each document. There are a number of prefettura offices throughout Italy that you can locate on the Internal Ministry site, Ministero dell'Interno. For Florence's prefettura office, it is located here:
    - <u>**Prefettura of Florence**</u>
      Ufficio Legalizzazione
      Via Giacomini 8
      Telephone: (+39) 055-278-3781
      Hours: Monday-Friday 9:00am-11:00am; Thursday 2:00pm- 4:00pm
      Fax: (+39) 055-278-3715
      Site: www.prefettura.it/firenze/multidip/index.htm

- **Schedule an appointment with the Marriage Office** in the town where you plan to be married to present all of your final documents. Again, if you get married directly in Florence you can do this at the following listed location, otherwise you can look it up in the town you have chosen. If you have chosen a small town to get married in and have written an email to get an appointment, with no response, it may help to translate it and send it over in Italian in case the worker or clerk on the other side does not read english, which can very well happen. It may even be good to provide them with scanned copies via email of everything you have obtained prior to receiving your final documents in Italy. They can look them over to see if you are on track retrieving everything that will be necessary.

- o **Florence City Hall** - Marriage Office
  Palazzo Vecchio – Palazzo della Signoria
  Telephone: (+39) 055-276-8518 or
  8370/8291/8276/8026
  Call Center: **055-055**
  Hours: Monday-Friday 8:30am-1:00pm; Tuesday
  2:30pm-5:00pm
  Site: www.comune.fi.it/export/sites/retecivica/

After the intent to marry is declared to the town hall, announcements are posted in the town where you will be married that notifies the public of the marriage. The length of time that these announcements are left up before the wedding varies and can be posted for up to two weeks delaying the marriage. If you are both non-Italian citizens, this part is waived and you get a freebie on your checklist.

All of your documents that we discussed above that are obtained within your country of origin must be legalized and translated to Italian by a certified translator. Your local Italian Consular office can provide you with a list of translators in your area. The legal documents that I mentioned that need an apostille stamp is because this authenticates the legality of the document to be recognized in foreign countries. These documents are only valid for 6 months so don't get them too far in advance. The apostille can be obtained at your Secretary of State's office via mail or in person. Again, if you are providing your originals by mail, I would take copies and allow yourself enough time to obtain them again in case of an accident of being lost in the mail.

Once you are married in Italy with a civil and/or religious ceremony, it will be recognized in your country of origin, but prior to leaving Italy make sure to receive an apostille stamp through the prefettura office of the area/town of where you were married. Also, check with your local town hall back home to make sure you understand what they will require and that you have all their needs before leaving Italy.

Depending on which wedding ceremony you choose, there are additional documents needed for religious ceremonies so please see the chapter on types of wedding ceremonies.

Sourced by: www.Italy.usaembassy.gov

Types of Wedding Ceremonies

There are three types of wedding ceremonies to consider for your wedding in Italy:
- Civil
- Religious
- Symbolic

Symbolic Weddings
The easiest of the three wedding ceremonies from a legality standpoint and the most flexible is the symbolic wedding. These are conducted by a celebrant, but it's doesn't legally marry you in Italy. This is an option for folks that get married in their own country and want to have a non-legally binding ceremony at their own desired location without all the legal document requirements, as this part has already been completed in your home country. If there are parts of your wedding day that are important to your culture that you want to incorporate, that aren't allowed in other ceremonies, this is your best option. Be as creative as you like as you make the rules about exactly how you want your day to be.

Civil Weddings
I chose a civil ceremony for the simple fact that I could legally get married in Italy and also have a wedding put together with details of how exactly I would want it. The civil ceremony is a legally binding ceremony and can be held at the town hall where you may be married by the mayor, as I was, or his deputies. It can also take place at a venue as well and, for an extra cost, the mayor will also attend to do the formal ceremony there. The venue will have their own fees for renting out the establishment and the town hall fees vary depending on the city. In Florence, for example, the rental fee for the marriage hall can range from a minimum of €750 to a maximum of €5,000 depending on the season and the day of the week you choose. If you chose Siena it will cost you about 700-800 euro, while the town I got married in within Bucine was only 150 euro. So, as you can see, there are large differences in your ceremony cost based on your selection.

Town Hall of Bucine

Married by the Mayor of Bucine

Translators

During the civil wedding ceremony, you will need two witnesses since they will need to sign a legal document as part of the ceremony. An interpreter is required to be present if you are non-Italian speaking and I highly recommend the interpreter that I used, Camilla Pedersen who can reached at camillapedersen@virgilio.it. A good majority of what she does is serving as a tour guide, but a part of her business is also assisting customers as a wedding planner. I used her services as a translator on our wedding day and if I could do it all again, I wouldn't hesitate using her services. She even allowed me to bounce some other legal questions off of her and assisted with other small aspects free of charge. Typically hiring a translator can cost you about 400 euro including translation of the documents before the ceremony in Italy. Camilla was very reasonable and I paid a little more than half of that cost including her depositing the documents at the local town hall in Italy where I was to be married. In Bucine, it meant meeting at the public town hall 2-3 days before the wedding to sign the last documents, submit all final documents and her translation services during the wedding. Very reasonable!

Another option if you are looking to save money is to contact a university local to where you'll be getting married and see if their language or english department has students or professors that are interested in making money on the side. If you happen to have family or a friend that can translate during the ceremony, that is acceptable. They have to make sure they know which documents need to be translated and they will need to sign off on the official translation of the documents. If you do this, the translator cannot be the same as your witness during the wedding ceremony.

Religious Ceremony
The most challenging wedding ceremony to conduct in Italy being a non-Italian is a religious ceremony. A religious ceremony is conducted by a Roman Catholic priest whom will register the marriage with the civil authorities. For a Roman Catholic wedding the church requires a whole other set of additional documents in addition to what we have already discussed. Not all Italian priests will conduct a religious wedding ceremony in Italy. Question your local priest first and maybe even your archbishop for some suggestions of whom they are aware of or whom they recommend you reach out to for such a ceremony in Italy. If you choose to be married by a non-Roman Catholic priest, it's possible that you may have to be married via a civil ceremony first. Check with your local priest as well as the priest at the church in Italy of your choice. Here are the requirements for a Roman Catholic wedding:

- A formal letter from your priest providing permission for you to be married in the church you select in Italy. It must state on the church's letterhead that the priest from your home church allows you to get married at the name of that particular church in Italy on the stated scheduled date. His letter should also include that you completed all Pre Cana requirements and if they provide a certificate demonstrating that a copy should be included.
- The same letter that your priest is writing should also be written by your bishop. These are requirements of the Italian Curia. The bishop's letter should state that there are not impediments to you getting married at the name of the particular church in Italy on that particular stated date.
- Include the original prenuptial inquiry form that you submitted to your church and filled out with your priest. It will have the priest's signature as his approval. Once that is completed, it must be stamped and sealed by the bishop as it proves to the Italian Curia that it has been

approved by a higher authority.
- Include all original certificates of baptism, first communion and confirmation. If those can't be located or obtained, get copies and make sure that they are stamped and sealed by the bishop as this is the most important part.
- If you are getting married by the Italian priest both civilly and religiously, then you need to perform the civil wedding first and provide the original civil wedding certificate to the priest.
- In the case that you have been divorced, the Catholic Church will not remarry you unless you have legally had your previous marriage annulled and then you will need to provide a civil reconciliation certificate.
- If one of you is not Catholic, you can still get married in the Catholic Church, but you must obtain a document/certificate named "permission of mixed religion" that has to be sealed and stamped by the bishop that states that you are allowed to be married by the Italian Catholic church. Discuss this with your local priest.

These religious documents should not be obtained more than 3 months in advance or they will expire except for your previously obtained certificates of baptism, first communion and confirmation. At least a month before the wedding, these documents should be sent to the Italian Curia. I suggest that you make sure you receive the Italian authorities approval before you provide all the originals. If they were to get lost you would need to resubmit all the originals and start all over again. Let's admit that this is probably the least fun part of the whole process.

The legalities are the most important aspect of planning your wedding in Italy so make sure to pay attention to every step and don't hesitate to reach out if you have questions.

The Food of Tuscany

Each region in Italy has their own cuisine and specialties and it's true when they say what grows together goes together when it comes to food and wine pairings. Food from Tuscany can be very simple, yet flavorful. I enjoy tasting the pure goodness of the fruits from the land, plus I'm a sucker for extra virgin Tuscan olive oil. There is nothing like fresh cold press olive oil with that slight greenish hue and in you are in the perfect region for experiencing this.

There are a number of foods to consider from this region when it comes to planning your wedding menu, but I wanted to provide some suggestions on the top appetizers, *antipasti*, 1st course, *primo piatto*, 2nd course, *secondo piatto,* and dessert, *dolce.* Be prepared to sit down and enjoy your wedding meal for hours. I've eaten in Italy for 3 hours before, but our wedding meal was literally 4 hours and the food just kept coming. We chose a local restaurant, Alla Corte di Bacco, in a nearby town from where we got married, the town of Ambra. We made sure to have dinner there earlier in the week and the food was outstanding. We knew from looking over the reviews online prior to our trip that this restaurant was probably going to be a great selection for our wedding dinner. After finishing our meal we discussed it with the owner and he reserved the room upstairs for us the evening of our wedding. I fully trusted, based on what we ate and our experience nights before, that they would prepare a typical Tuscan meal to everyone's liking. They even requested that since they get their fish fresh daily, if there were folks in our party that were fish lovers, they would organize a fish feast for those interested. After all, folks do go to Italy to eat so when you're in a local restaurant with authentic food, I have enough trust in the cook to know what goes best to prepare for our guests and ourselves at such a special event.

You can always reach out to a restaurant in advance as well if they have contact information on their site rather than waiting until you get there. If it's a local restaurant to where you will be staying, which I'm assuming it would be, you can also request that your accommodations make the reservation for you as well. The benefit of just ordering off the menu in a restaurant is that everyone can order what they like as opposed to the venues or caterers that are going to charge you a set price per person.

The restaurant or venue and caterer you chose will obviously provide you with their own selections, but this should give you an idea of some typical Tuscan cuisine to consider.

Appetizer ~ *L'antipasto*
Figs, *fichi*
Melon & prosciutto, *melone e prosciutto*
cured meats, *I salami*
porcini mushrooms, *funghi porcini*
chestnuts, *castagne*
truffles, *tartufi*
typical cheese platter – pecorino, caprino, stracchino, etc.
crostini with chicken liver pate, *crostini con pate di fegato di pollo*

1st course ~ *Primo piatto*
Ribollita soup
Bruschetta
Tortelli or ravioli with butter and sage, *tortelli con burro e salvia*
Pappardelle or tagliatelle with wild boar, duck or hare, *pappardelle con cinghiale, anatra o lepre*
Panzanella (stale bread with tomato, basil and onion)

2nd course ~ *Secondo piatto*
The prized *bistecca alla fiorentina* from the chianina cows
chicken, *pollo*
wild boar, *cinghiale*
wild hare, *lepre*
sausage, *salsiccia*
rabbit, *coniglio*

Dessert ~ *Dolce*
Biscotti, *contucci*, with vin santo (liqueur)
tiramisu
limoncello (after dinner drink made with lemons)

geleto or sorbet, *sorbetto*

Wedding Cake

Today many versions of wedding cakes exist from the multiple tiered cakes all the way down to wedding cupcakes. Italy has its own traditional wedding cakes and if you want to follow more traditional style, here are some Italian specialties you should consider.

Millefoglie – This is one of the most popular options, literally translating to "thousand layers". It's a cake made of filo pastry layers with marscapone and cream and is usually a one layer cake topped with icing and maybe some berries. This was what we had at our wedding as a surprise offered by the restaurant. I had researched my options, but knowing all too well the dinners in Italy, I figured we would enjoy the house dolce specialties if there was even any room left in our bellies.

Crostata di Frutta – Most likely known as a fruit tart in the states, it's a single layer custard tart topped with berries.

Gelato or Sorbet– Especially in the hot temperatures of the summer months, this is always a pleasant and refreshing end to a meal.

Catering Services

Depending upon your selection of a venue will determine if you will need to seek out a caterer. Most venues have caterers that they use regularly and recommend. This is something to consider as it will make your life easier. If you choose to bring in your own caterer, you may find that you have to pay an extra fee to the venue. If you need to seek out catering services I found the website, In Italy Wedding, to be useful as it includes a number of long standing caterers in business with price ranges and the services they cover. You can also search on different locations and sections of Tuscany. It's a one stop shop website for a do-it-yourself wedding. Check with your venue and caterer as well to make sure items such as linens and lighting are included.

When you begin to reach out to potential vendors, challenge them. Provide them exactly with all your needs and what you are looking for. It wouldn't hurt to ask them why they should be selected as the vendor to help you fulfill your wedding needs and desires. It may seem silly, but those vendors are there to make your day special. They care about their customers and should be more than happy to provide you with their mission and goals and the reason why they do what they do. You want companies that show customization and are willing to go the extra mile for you on your special day.

The Wines of Tuscany

Luckily, if you choose Tuscany to get married, you will have one of the most beautiful landscapes surrounded by vineyards and olive groves galore set along hillside after hillside. There is nothing like getting married along the Tuscan landscapes, nevermind, a Tuscan vineyard or just being able to drink wine straight from the source itself. It's a great activity, as well, for you and your guests to tour wineries and arrange wine tastings with the opportunity to meet the winemakers themselves. You can even set up luncheons at the wineries if you book in advance to really fulfill the Tuscan wine experience and provide even more memorable moments for you and your guests.

Being a certified Italian Wine Specialist and Italian wine blogger, I could go crazy sharing all the variety of wines from this region, but let's stick with what this region is well known for. When it comes to the top red grape, sangiovese, and the top white grape, vernaccia. The sangiovese grape is a red grape that is best known for making Chianti in Tuscany. A clone of the sangiovese grape makes up two of the top wines of Tuscany and Italy's top list of wines; Brunello di Montalcino from the town of Montalcino in Tuscany and Vino Nobile di Montepulciano from the town of Montepulciano in Tuscany. The highlighted white wine of this region, Vernaccia di San Gimignano, is from the town of San Gimignano in Tuscany. You also have the choice of the white grape, vermentino, which is the best from the Maremma in southern Tuscany as well as the worldly prized "Super Tuscan" red wines of Tuscany. It is typically a blend of international varieties of cabernet sauvignon and merlot with sangiovese, although there are many variations of the wines.

For the photographer in you that loves vineyard shots, one of the best roads to drive down that takes you right through the heart of the Chianti Classico zone is the SS222, known as the Chiantigiana. When you have seen pictures of vineyards in the Tuscan hillside, there is a good chance that they were shot on this road or in this area. It's full of windy roads lined with olive groves, cypress trees, vineyards and hilltop towns with ancient medieval buildings. This was the road I chose to have our shuttle drive down the day of our wedding, as I wanted to make sure that I stopped to get some unique picture settings. After all, I am an Italian wine blogger so of course I had to have shots in the vineyards themselves. Nothing like hiking up your dress and getting right into the thick of things. This was during harvest time as well when I was there in October so some grapes were still on the vines, which you may want to keep in mind if you want grapes in the pictures. Many wineries pick by end of September to October depending on the grapes they grow and the weather that season.

Along the Chiantigiana

In addition to wine, before and during the meal, many Italians complete their meals with one of the most popular liqueurs, limoncello. I actually made limoncello for the first time to hand out as gifts for our wedding guests as it's rather simple to make including only lemons, sugar and alcohol. Another after dinner drink in Tuscany, that I mentioned earlier, is vin santo, a fortified dessert wine made typically of the trebbiano and malvasia white grapes.

Barrels of Vin Santo

To brush up on your Italian wine knowledge specifically within Tuscany, I have a number of articles on wineries that I have visited there and on the wines of the region on my website Vino Travels.

Wedding Attire & Aethetics

I'm certainly not one of those women that has dreamed about her wedding day since the day I was born nor had every ounce of my wedding day planned out from the theme to the colors, cake or the dress. Every woman wants to make sure she looks and feels the best she has ever felt so everything including your dress, hair, makeup, shoes and accessories are all important items. Finding "the dress" is one of the biggest, if not the biggest, item on your wedding agenda. Luckily, this is the fun part and a great time to share memories with your girlfriends, family and above all your mother. Since this will most likely be done in your home country, my suggestion is to make sure to try on styles outside of what you have in mind. You may be surprised at what looks flattering on you compared to what you think. That's what happened to me and what I thought I was getting is different than what I actually decided on.

The time of year and month you choose to get married in Tuscany dictates the weather conditions, which can influence, to a certain degree, your wedding attire. You obviously want to be glamorous that day, but comfortable. With temperatures in July and August being quite hot, you may want to consider certain materials depending on how heavy they are. Of course no one can plan for weather, but you can be prepared. Plan for rain, warm weather even gelato stains. Oh yes, this is Italy and if you're roaming around towns it can happen. Ask my wedding dress. While we were venturing through the Tuscan countryside on our shuttle, we stopped in the town of Castellina in Chianti for a refreshing gelato break and somehow, when we got back on the shuttle, a red dot of gelato was on my wedding gown even though I wasn't even eating any. You are in Italy after all so when I say plan for everything, I mean plan for everything. Traipsing through Italian vineyards could mean dirt or grape stains. Although, it's difficult to get upset in midst of all the beauty and aspects of Tuscan living surrounding you so just go with it and maybe be a little prepared with some seltzer water or a tide stick.

Something to consider while you are venturing over to Italy in advance to check out your venues and meet vendors is to consider purchasing your wedding dress in Italy. This would have been something I would have loved to have done if I made a trip prior to the wedding. You can always get your alterations done at home.

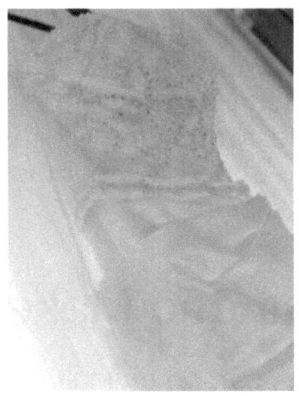

What about the journey the dress endures to get to your final Italian destination safely? I wouldn't recommend shipping your dress as that concern of doubt lingers about whether or not it will make it there and you don't want to put yourself in that situation. Depending on the size of your dress, it may be a little cumbersome to trudge it through the airport. I carried mine with me as a carry-on through the airport. I had a satin mermaid style dress so it wasn't as heavy or large as a princess ballgown style, which may be a little more challenging and burdensome. All the on-flight crews I encountered aboard the aircrafts were very helpful when boarding and many took it to hang in their closet or first class space even though I was in coach. Just ask prior to boarding or while boarding the flight. Once you finally reach your destination, make sure to hang your dress up to let any creases or wrinkles out. Hanging it in the bathroom and running a hot shower to create steam is a perfect and easy solution to get them out.

You can make your wedding day as elegant and formal or more on the casual side as you desire. This is Italy though and is one of the top fashionable countries of the world. Not only the women, but the men are dressed to the nines as well. Make sure your guests are aware, if you chose to get married in an Italian church that baring your shoulders or knees is not permitted. Make sure to have something to put over your shoulders. If you're a female think of the shoes on your feet as you will most likely be walking through some very ancient, cobblestone roads and they aren't the easiest to walk on for those with the lesser trained feet compared to the everyday Italian citizen. I remember when I lived there back in 2001 and watched the everyday woman walking on high heels on those streets without hesitation like it was no big deal. You don't want to look like you're super wobbly on your wedding day or always be looking down at the street. Remember to shine those pearly whites and look up for pictures.

Hair and Makeup

Professional hair styles can be difficult to achieve on one's own. A hairdresser these days can typically cost you about 300-400 euro including a trial and styling the day of the wedding, nevermind getting a makeup artist as well. I was actually pretty shocked by the cost of hair stylists when performing research. With the internet though, anything is possible. If you're trying to save and with a little bit of creativity you can explore other options that I'll mention. The larger the town or city the more options you will have. For example, if you are getting married in Florence you can google hair salons in Florence Italy and will be provided with websites to some salons located in Florence with contact information, ie, Contrasto Salone (An Aveda salon), BH

Salon and Contesta Rock Hair. Any website that doesn't have a translation as well can be translated via web translation tools. It may be good to reach out to the salon and send over some pictures of what you would like done and get some prices. If you are money conscious as I was, there are hair schools that you can contact in Florence as I did including Academy F. They can recommend students or even professors that will travel at a certain cost for outside jobs.

The same goes for makeup artists. When I was researching makeup artists, I reached out to Pop Makeup Academy in Florence. I have also read great reviews on Adrienne Aereboe who is a bridal makeup artist and hair stylist. You can locate reviews online as well as all her contact information as well as makeup artist, Janita Helova. If you're going to hire a hairstylist or makeup artist, ask for their portfolio or browse their website and social media pages if they have them to get an idea of their work.

Try also contacting someone from your accommodations about whom they recommend and see if they can get you some contacts. If the overall cost of the hairstyle is too much for you and you have some time in Italy prior to the wedding, there is another idea. Try walking into a salon, make an appointment without mentioning the word "wedding" and you'll pay a fraction of the price for the same quality hairdo. Depending on how much you trust yourself, you can always go to a well-known makeup store like a Sephora and they usually are always willing to do trials and teach you some tricks of the trade either free or for a low cost. This is an easy way to learn how to do it yourself and save lots of money, maybe even pick up some new makeup for the wedding. As far as the men, well they have it too easy. There isn't too much that they screw up unless they are super picky about their style, but regardless it's a lot easier to manage on a wedding day than for females, as we all know.

If you won't be in Florence for your wedding, you can search for folks the same way. Some of the people recommended from the schools will travel as well as the stylists or artists that you choose, but you'll have to pay for that if you want them to come to you. Remember, a villa or residence that you will be staying at would be more than willing to provide suggestions and as you select wedding vendors, they may also know folks from working in the industry.

Musical Offerings

Music is one of those things that can either make or break your wedding and completely set the mood. Along with the food at a wedding, the music played at a wedding creates one of the memorable aspects of a wedding that guests will remember. Some questions to ask yourself are:

- Are you going to want a band, a string quartet, harpist, pianist or maybe a DJ or even nothing at all but a CD?
- How long are you going to need their services including during the ceremony, cocktail hour, dinner and following dinner for dancing?

If you'll be getting married in a church they most likely have their own pianist or other musicians that you could also consider. Maybe these folks will be willing to be hired for the ceremony or at least a part of it like the cocktail hour and dinner time. If you need something more lively following dinner consider your DJ, bands or a CD that you've made yourself with your own selections. Your entertainment should know, but every town varies in terms of their noise ordinances and how late music can be played at the venue itself within that town so make sure to check.

When I think of Italy and weddings for some reason I think of musicians playing musical instruments on a beautiful grass filled villa in the countryside. A two man band that comes highly recommended from a number of different weddings that were hosted in Tuscany are Guty e Simone. They may be slightly priced higher than some other options, but are highly professional and are very accommodating to the bride and grooms requests and play music that really get you up and dance.

Music license
If you are hiring entertainment to play music at your wedding you will need to purchase an SIAE license. This is required by Italian law as they request that you receive this license for when intellectual property is exploited. Check with your vendor to see

if that is included or will be an extra expense. If your vendor states that it's not necessary you should purchase it regardless. It costs about 79 euro if you have less than 200 guests and 119 euro if greater than 200 guests. Once you have obtained your license and paid your fee you will receive a receipt from the authority, ENPALS. Make sure to keep your receipt as proof of payment to bring to the wedding. If the authorities were to show up it can definitely put a damper on the event and cause a scene. You can read further about it at their website if you read Italian, www.siae.it, or have it translated.

Selecting a Photographer

Other than selecting a location and dress, selecting a photographer was one of my biggest decisions. These will be your visual memories forever and bragging rights to your friends to show them your dream wedding in Italy. I used a particular site that was perfect in helping to choose the right photographer. The website is the International Society of Professional Wedding Photographers, ISPWP. The site provides information on photographers from all around the world that you can narrow down specifically to Italy. There is a large list, but I browsed through the price range first along with the regions that they service. From there, I started browsing through some of their portfolios and websites to see if their style of picture taking and quality of pictures is what I was aiming for. It looks very overwhelming at first, but once I started looking at some of the pictures, I knew whether or not I wanted to contact some photographers further.

Make sure to consider the full packages each individual photographer is offering as some may include an album where others may charge a premium for it. Is there editing or touching up the photos? Does it include a DVD of the pictures or is that extra? This will help you determine the overall value of each individual photographer's packages.

For my wedding photographer, I chose Domenico Costabile and was satisfied with his services. You'll see many of his photographs as well throughout this book. Make sure that the photographer you choose can speak your language or that there is someone there that can translate. It will be difficult to communicate during the sessions about what exactly they want you to do if there isn't that communication. This can be detected easily overseas by setting up a skype session and meeting each other face-to-face over the computer before selecting your vendor. Thank goodness for technology!

Prior to signing any contracts, don't hesitate to ask for contact information for some of their previous clients. I did this and spoke with one of the previous customers to question their experience, if you sensed any red flags, and what their comments were on the photographer's services. Plus, it provides you with some ease about paying for these services in advance by knowing that you have spoken with someone whom has used their services. When you get to the point of signing a contract and sending payments to reserve your selected photography service I find Paypal is a good way of exchanging money as they have many policies in place to protect you as a buyer and the vendor as a seller. Make sure you read the fine print and details before ever signing any contract or sending any payment.

Choosing a Florist

Flower pieces can be very simple to complex bouquets and either have a romantic elegance or a rustic charm. Depending upon your needs a typical bouquet can cost you around 75-100 euro. The long list of potential flower needs include the bride's bouquet, the man's boutonnieres, corsages and if you have your wedding party with you, then you'll want to consider their arrangements. Do you also want flowers for the ceremony on tables, in the church, decorated arches, hair pieces?

Many towns have beautiful florist shops and depending on how early you are heading over to Italy, in advance of the wedding, it may be enough preparation for them to get something together, but obviously the more demand you have the more time will be required to put something together. If you're staying at a villa or residence in the countryside, you can always send over pictures of what you want and see if they can help. These local towns are all about supporting their locals businesses and would love to give some business to a local shop in town for someone celebrating their marriage. If it's a very tiny town, as the one where I got married in, you may have difficulty finding a florist shop so look to your closest larger town and start there.

Of course Tuscany is known for its sunflowers and you may dream of getting your pictures in those endless fields of sunflowers. If that's the case, you'll want to plan on getting married there in June to July, but this is dependent upon the weather for that year. It may start slightly earlier at the end of May or later into August.

We didn't personally have our wedding party with us and we chose to keep it intimate with our immediate families, so we just made sure I had a wedding bouquet of what I feel represents Tuscany's finest, sunflowers. I kept it real simple and was very impressed how beautiful simplicity can be in Italy. Before the wedding we were traveling as a family to visit some local Tuscan towns. Where better than to visit the famous town of Cortona that has made so many folks fall in love with Tuscany via the movie by Frances Mayes "Under the Tuscan Sun". In the center of town was a local florist shop and when I saw those big, bright yellow sunflower heads with beautiful long green stems I knew that was going to be it. They wrapped them up with some beautiful yellow ribbon and I was perfectly content. It was simple, but perfect. Dare I tell you it only cost me about 5-6 euro? Granted I'm a lot more simple than most, but you can't get any better than the big, gorgeous, bright yellow sunflowers of Tuscany.

For a great overview of what flowers are in season during certain times of the year check out Exclusive Italy Weddings as they offer a chart on their website.

ENJOY YOUR WEDDING PLANNING IN TUSCANY AND CONGRATS!

www.ingramcontent.com/pod-product-compliance
Lightning Source LLC
Chambersburg PA
CBHW050508290526
45786CB00006B/2488